THE BOOK OF
BE ATTITUDES
A Treasury of Positive Behaviors and Sage Advice

Bob "BB" Baumann

D1354663

A PERIGEE BOOK

Perigee Books
are published by
The Putnam Publishing Group
200 Madison Avenue
New York, NY 10016

Library of Congress Cataloging-in-Publication Data
Baumann, Bob, date.
The book of be attitudes : a treasury of positive behaviors
and sage advice / Bob Baumann.
p.   cm.
1. Conduct of life—Quotations, maxims, etc.   I. Title.
BJ1581.2.B36 1992   92-9483   CIP
170'.44—dc20

ISBN 0-399-51787-1

Cover design by Mike McIver

Book design by Rhea Braunstein

Printed in the United States of America
1 2 3 4 5 6 7 8 9 10

This book is printed on acid-free paper.

This book is dedicated to
You.

THE BOOK OF
BE ATTITUDES

Preface

As a child, I heard my parents tell me to go to my room until I changed my attitude. "But what did they mean by that?" I often wondered to myself. What is an attitude? How can I change my attitude? I usually found myself sitting in my room, mystified, waiting for my parents to change *their* attitude.

As an adult, I found that physical behavior was a reflection of mental attitudes. What I needed in order to behave more successfully was a wardrobe of attractive, effective, and positive attitudes. I could then dress my mental self with my choices.

Having the concept of "Be Attitudes" available to me over a long period of time has greatly influenced the quality of my life. My outlook in general has improved, my relationships are most enjoyable, and others find attractive attitudes infectious. It rubs off on them. And, by the way, it's wonderful to live, work, and play with people who have such great attitudes.

This book contains treasures of positive attitudes from the English language. Thought-provoking phrases and sage advice follow each ''Be Attitude'' to nurture the spirit and spark the imagination. Fill your mind with uplifting thoughts and embark upon a life journey of well being.

Step inside each one of these attitudes. Try them on. Feel the part. Experience the multitude of choices available to you at any given moment. Scan the selections often. Make up your own. Memorize them. Practice them. And positively accept being who you are, as you choose to be.

A

BE ABLE
Do for yourself
all that you are capable of doing.
Only then will other people gladly assist you
should you need further help.

BE ABUNDANT
Count your blessings as they occur.
Periodically take inventory
of the ways in which you are fortunate.

BE ACTING
The word act is the root word
for the word PRACTICE.
It is the first step
in making something happen.
But beware,
it is also a kindred soul of REACTION.

BE ADEPT
Cultivate a refined sense of ability.
Create confidence with your skills and talents.
Seek to be first-rate and proficient.

BE ADJUSTING
Life is constantly changing,
so make accommodations.
Intention is your steering wheel
to stay safely on the road.

BE AESTHETIC
Variety is essential to the concept of beauty.
Take the contrasts you find in life
and unify them with your sense of harmony.

BE AFFABLE
The presence of a friend
enhances enjoyment and promotes goodwill.
Invite the opportunity to share affinities.
Be likeable.

BE AFFECTIONATE

Touch another in a loving manner.
Continue to attend to your relationships
with sincere, heartfelt endearments.

BE AFFIRMATIVE

Establish your ideas with confidence
and edify belief in the goodness
you look forward to.
Assert your worthiness.

BE AGELESS

Live in the here and now.
Do not restrict yourself to a chronological age.

BE AGILE

Move with the grace of your personal expression,
in your own timing.

BE ALIGNED

Focus on what matters most,
and synchronize your thoughts, feelings,
and actions.

BE ALLAYED

Relax,
put your unreal fears to rest.

BE ALLOWING

Give yourself and others
space to make time and time to make space.
Let your patience be so strong
that you can let others be first if necessary.

BE ALLURING

Let your essence come forth
and disclose irresistible appeal.
Arouse magnetic fascination
with an attractively charming personality.

BE ALTRUISTIC

Be thankful for those who gave their lives
in order that you could have
a better chance than they had
when they were born.
Always be concerned
with the welfare of our children's children.

BE AMAZED

Enjoy the surprise you feel
upon finding the answers or solutions you seek.
Take delight
in what you find awe-inspiring.
Marvel at the breathless wonders of life,
and the universe we live in.

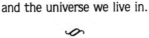

BE AMBITIOUS

Be eager and bold to unleash the power
of reaching for your dreams.
Experience the passion of your enthusiasm.

BE AMIABLE
Be playfully loving
in your personal relationships.
Remain affectionate, easygoing, and gentle.

BE AMOROUS
Predispose yourself to love.
In doing so,
a flood of similar feelings
make themselves available to you,
for instance;
friendliness, kindness, encouragement, passion.

BE AMUSING
Elicit happiness
with laughter and good cheer,
pleasantly and unexpectedly,
bringing joy to others.
Emanate the gentle light-ness of life.

BE ANTICIPATING
Relish the elixir of hope and optimism.
Savor the delicious adventure of expectation.
Enjoy the excursion
of looking forward to your dreams.

BE APPEALING
Promote
that which has real and eternal value
within you.
Garnish your attractiveness
with truth, beauty, and goodness.

BE APPRAISING
It is especially important
to affectionately and vocally
estimate the nature and value
of children, family, friends, and associates.
Your comments
are often the cornerstones of their beliefs.

BE APPRECIATIVE
That which you feel and show admiration for
multiplies and grows more valuable over time.
Escalate your worth and meaning,
as you develop your mind.

BE APPROACHABLE
Be easy to talk with and pleasant to know.
Allow your unfolding personality to be accessible
with all of its emotions and intelligence.

BE ARTICULATE
Present your ideas with clarity.
Formulate your thoughts
and speak your mind effectively.
Learn to use language
easily and fluently.

BE ARTISTIC

Show skill and excellence in all your art forms
whatever they may be.
Exhibit taste
with discriminating judgment and sensitivity.

BE ASCENDING

In all your endeavors,
move to a higher ground.
Go back in time and remember.

BE ASKING

It isn't dumb to ask questions,
but it would be dumb if you didn't.
Don't be afraid to ask.

BE ASPIRING

Be eagerly desirous,
especially for something great or of a high value.
Give yourself permission
to go after what you most desire.

BE ASSERTIVE

Honestly promote your opinions
and your actions
by placing your footing
on the firm ground of your self-esteem.
Act in ways that enhance your self-respect
and watch others respond accordingly.

BE ASSISTING

Be present in your life
to give support and aid
to someone else who needs it.
Be available physically, emotionally,
and spiritually.

BE ASSOCIATING

Relate peace with prosperity.
Bring into relationship
your thoughts, feelings, and memories,
as a means of creating
value and perspective in your life.
Connect giving with receiving.

BE ASTUTE

Cultivate in your heart and mind
a flair for discerning the truth.
Be ingenious in your creativity
and clever in your actions.

BE ATHLETIC

The art of physical action
generates strength of character
and bears the fruit of a well-nourished spirit.
Engage in activities which cause you to grow.
And remember, you will always be
your own best competition.

BE ATTAINING

Know that each second going by
represents what you set in motion long ago.
You are already reaching,
achieving,
and accomplishing every moment.
The key to being what you want to be
is to live the life you seek in the first place.

BE ATTENTIVE

Attention is a mental energy force.
The success of your intentions
depends on your ability
to use this magnificent energy.
Focus it.

BE ATTITUDINAL

Develop a philosophy
of artfully manipulating your approaches
to the problems and challenges you find in life.

BE ATTRACTIVE

Produce pleasure and delight
for yourself and those around you
with a presence of beauty vibrating with appeal.
Aesthetic forms and ideas decorate your body,
mind,
and spirit
according to your considerations of quality.

BE ATTRIBUTIVE
Qualify your experience
with positive adjectives, descriptive words,
and inspiring phrases.
Ascribe your successes
to your ability of making up your mind.
As you make up your mind,
so, too do you make up your world.

BE AUSPICIOUS
Recognize each moment
as being opportune, favorable, and propitious.
Decide to make the best of things
by looking for the best of things.

BE AUTHENTIC
Be genuine and real.
Others will treat you as reliable and trustworthy
and entitled to acceptance and belief
because of your alignment
with known facts and experience.

BE AUTONOMOUS

The one who conquers self
has conquered the world.
If you don't choose to do this,
others will do it for you.
Operate under your own will power.

BE AVAILABLE

Be suitable and ready for use.
Be present in your life
for yourself and others.
And be accessible emotionally
in order that it not be a lonely journey.

BE AWAKE

Maintain a clear-headed awareness
of what's going on immediately around you.
Be attentive and alert.

BE AWARE

Be mindful and knowledgeable,
ready to respond
to the known and the unknown.
Consciously acknowledge your life
and make the best of it.

B

BE BALANCED
Great peace of mind can be attained
when perspective has been adjusted
to harmonious proportions.
Stability is an ever-changing series of events,
however,
so remain ready to make adjustments.

BE BEATIFIC
Bestow bliss, blessings, and happiness
upon others.

BE BEAUTIFUL
That which is beautiful
has excellence of form, color, and presence.
Beauty includes the noble and spiritual qualities
of being you to the fullest.

BE BEAUTIFYING

Fashion, form, and mold your dreams and ideals.
Take what you find in life and sculpture it
according to your sense of loveliness and grace.

BE BECOMING

Take time in becoming who you are.
Unfold
according to your internal sense of growth.
And, in your processes of change,
take care when tending the garden
of your being.

BE BEING

Be a human being,
not a human doing,
or a human having.
Possess the essence of personal presence.

BE BELIEVING

Have confidence in the truth within you.
And, as you shine the light
of your faith and intelligence,
the truth will indeed set you free.

BE BENEVOLENT

Do good or cause good to be done.
Be tender and loving in action and purpose.
"Volent" means voluntary
and "bene" means good.
Be voluntarily good.

BE BENIGN

Be gracious and have a kind disposition.
Be favorable through your gentleness.
Bestow the best you can on yourself and others.

BE BETTER

You don't have to be sick to get better,
because there is always room for improvement.
Remember, not better than,
just better.

∽

BE BLESSED

Be blissfully happy and contented,
knowing that you are worthy of being happy.
You were created to be this way.

∽

BE BLOOMING

Unfold in your life like a flower.
Allow yourself to establish your roots,
find nourishment,
create the structure of your stem,
send forth your leaves to receive light,
blossom exuberantly with the colors
of your petals,
and, smile!

BE BONDING
Create strong and enduring qualities of affection
Bond without bondage.
Explore affinity with another.

BE BOUNTEOUS
Be predisposed to give freely
and as you have freely given, receive.

BE BRAINSTORMING
Put your heads together.
Develop new ideas with others
and participate in solving problems
with unrestrained discussions.

BE BRAVE
Possess the person you are,
no one else will do it for you.
It is up to you.

BE BRIGHT

Be animated, lively, and cheerful.
First look to the light
as the source of your being,
and as you do so, others will see it too.
You reflect that which you concentrate on.
Polish yourself into a brilliant personality.

BE BRILLIANT

Find your talents,
and magnify them with your participation.

BE BUILDING

Engage in the art of molding your thoughts,
forming your system of thinking,
and creating plans
for constructing
your physical, emotional, and spiritual
environment.

BE BUOYANT

In the great ocean of life,
allow yourself
to always rise to the surface.
Bounce back from disappointments
and depression
and regain your posture.

C

BE CALM
Move serenely through your world
and give permission for a tranquil solution
to life's problems.
Be a mirror for others,
for through you
they too gain
a greater sense of peace of mind.

BE CANDID
Remain open, sincere, and spontaneous.
Let your affairs be filled
with heart-to-heart exchanges
and genuine humor.

BE CAPABLE
Have the diligence to utilize
your intelligence and ability
to accomplish that which you set your mind to.

BE CARESSING
Touch your world gently,
and with affection.
Integrate the gestures of fond attachment
with sensitivity and empathy.

BE CAUSE
Be the cause for something,
not just the effect.
Choose to be the master of your destiny
and the captain of your ship.

BE CELEBRATING
Observe this day
as the day you have waited for so long.
Choose to be happy.

BE CENTERED

Drive your life as from the middle of your bliss.
Be fueled with perspectives
which balance the good and bad.
Have a healthy approach to daily life.

BE CERTAIN

That which you passionately want in your heart
is truly possible.
Be free from doubt and reservations.

BE CHANGING

Attend the present
with an aptitude
for modifying your identity
toward a desirable future.

BE CHARISMATIC

Exercise a remarkable drawing power
over people
without dictatorship.
Inspire hope and confidence in the hearts
of those
you encounter.

BE CHARMING

Inspire others to join you in your journey,
by being who you are.
Continue to be sweet, delightful, and enjoyable.

BE CHEERFUL

Promote, express, and induce a pleasant mirth
when you are by yourself or with others.
Embody a hearty inclination
to work with optimism.

BE CHERISHING

Hold dearly that which you find valuable.
Care for tenderly those thoughts and things
which bring forth the pleasure of peace,
and the peace of pleasure.

BE CLEAR

Adjust your perspective
so that you can think without confusion,
see without distortion,
and speak powerfully.

BE CLEVER

Show inventiveness and originality.
Be mentally bright and utilize your intelligence.
Be skillful in character.

BE CLUED-IN
Be supplied with and use
that which serves to guide and direct you
in discovering solutions to your problems.
Use role models.

BE COEXISTING
Peacefully admit that you are part of a whole.
Act as though you belong to a family.

BE COHESIVE
Be a force
within the soul of humanity
which acts to unite its parts.

BE COLORFUL
Flavor life
with the spices of your personality.
Be rich in your imagination.
Display the rainbowlike spectrum
of your personal attributes.

BE COMFORTING

Soothe and console the people you care about.
Encourage them beyond these passing moments.
Think of ways to help them do
the things they cannot do for themselves.

BE COMICAL

Promote truly excellent causes and reasons
for genuine laughter.

BE COMMITTED

Entrust yourself to that which is worthy of you.
Empower your relationships
with the assurance of believable intentions.

BE COMMUNICATIVE
Defeat social alienation
by voicing your ideas
and sharing your viewpoint.
And remember, listening is a necessary part
of interacting with
those you communicate with.

BE COMPASSIONATE
Empathy desires the removal of the cause
for pain and suffering,
for yourself as well as others.
Compassion emanates
when you act on this desire.

BE COMPETENT
Ascend through the following for effective
accomplishment:
unconscious incompetence,
conscious incompetence,
conscious competence,
and unconscious competence.

BE COMPLIMENTARY

As you express your opinions to others,
commend them constructively
and foster their self-esteem.
Let your light shine.

BE COMPOSING

Artistically take
the elements of your surroundings
and synthesize them into an environment
which acts to combine
the elements of truth, beauty, and goodness.

BE COMPREHENSIBLE

Be understandable.
Use your intelligence.

BE CONCENTRATED

For more efficient efforts
focus your attention
and energize your emotions.

BE CONFIDENT
Believe in yourself.
Be assured that you are on firm ground.
Give yourself permission to be bold.

BE CONGRATULATING
Express pleasure and joy
for yourself and others
by recognizing special occasions
with your participation.

BE CONGRUENT
Bring
your physical, mental, and emotional natures
into alignment and harmony.
Empower yourself with this unity.

BE CONSCIENTIOUS
Have a sense of what is right or wrong
in your conduct and motives,
impelling you toward right action.

BE CONSCIOUS
Be "with thought,"
aware of what you are doing,
sensitive to the dialogue you are having
with yourself.

BE CONSIDERATE
Deliberately contemplate
and have regard for
other people's feelings and circumstances.

BE CONSISTENT
Steadfastly adhere
to your integrated principles, motives,
courses of action,
and forms of thought and feeling.

BE CONSOLING
Help to lessen
other people's grief, sorrow,
and disappointments;
reestablish a sense of solace and hope.

BE CONSTRUCTIVE
Seek to improve the world around you
with your actions, opinions, and comments.
You are responsible for building a future
that can stand up to your criticism.

BE CONTENT
Be satisfied now
and you will always know how
to be satisfied.

BE COOPERATIVE
Be willing to work and act together
for a common purpose,
in harmony.

BE COSMOPOLITAN
Be a citizen of the earth.

BE COURAGEOUS
Be encouraged and know
that the universe supports your success.

BE CREATIVE
Be original
in your thinking and expressions.
Be ingenious with your imagination.
Tap into a preverbal frame of mind
and feel your way into notions
which have never been before.

BE CULTIVATING
Promote the growth and development
of that which serves to bring success.
Labor for the harvest
of truth, beauty, and goodness.

BE CULTURED

Acquaint yourself
with that which is regarded as excellent.
Don't limit yourself to the known.
Be curious to see new insights and beauty
in that which is valid
in arts, letters, science,
and pursuits which are foreign to you.

BE CURIOUS

Be inquisitive,
desiring to learn and know.

D

BE DARING
Have the necessary courage to be
and do something you desire.

BE DAUNTLESS
Have purpose and fear nothing.
Your boldness
is kindred to your genius.

BE DECENT
Conform to the culturally recognized standards
of propriety, good taste, and modesty.
Be worthy of being respected.

BE DECISIVE
Engage your power of determination
and display your ability to choose.
Be free from ambiguity and hesitation.
Resolve your determination
to pursue your goals.

BE DECLARATIVE
Reveal your position to others.
Tell them what you want,
and enlist their enthusiasm for your success.

BE DECORATIVE
Enhance your environment
according to personal taste.
Furnish and adorn your life with beauty.

BE DELIGHTED
Be highly pleased
with that which is worthy of you.
Happiness is its own reward.

BE DELIGHTFUL
Be responsible for the atmosphere
you surround yourself with.
Afford pleasure and happiness to those you love.

BE DESIGNING
Use forethought to put your life in order.
Express an artistic nature.
Arrange your aspirations.

BE DESIRABLE
Be excellent and worth desiring.
Be pleasing and fine for yourself first.
Finish your posture with a smile.

BE DETERMINED
Be unwaveringly decided.
Persist in your choices.
Go for it.

BE DEVELOPING

Grow
into a more mature and
advanced state of being.
Elaborate
on your talents and expand your horizons.
Increase
your propensity to bloom at any age.

BE DEXTEROUS

Apply available skills
and develop the usage of your hands, body,
and mind.

BE DIFFERENT

Know that no one is identical
and enjoy your distinctions.

BE DILIGENT
Be constant
in your efforts to accomplish something.
Pursue your goals with persevering attention.

BE DISCERNING
Mentally distinguish
the truth, beauty, and goodness
of your life.

BE DOING
Action is an integral part of being.
Performance and execution are both important
to manifesting your desires.

BE DRAMATIC
Act out the character you are.
Cast yourself into roles
which you regard as highly effective
in expression.

BE DREAMING

Indulge in your dreams
and your aspirations.
Lucidly imagine a bright future
and happy occasions.
Enhance your endeavors with visionary clarity.

BE DYNAMIC

Explode with enthusiasm
and exude the essence of activity.
Empower your self-esteem
with effervescent emotions.

E

BE EASY
Let your disposition
reflect an attitude of co-operation.
Get along with others
and don't take things too seriously.

BE EBULLIENT
Be high-spirited.
Let the fervor of your enthusiasm
bubble over
with the excitement you feel.

BE ECLECTIC
Select and use
what you consider are the best elements
of any system
of medicine, philosophy or culture.

BE ECSTATIC
Let your emotions embrace and express
the rapturous delight you feel
when all is right
or becoming that way.

BE EDIFYING
Be a force which uplifts
and increases the faith and constitution
of your family and friends.

BE EDUCATED
Receive instruction from the schooling available
by drawing upon your natural intelligence
and willingness to learn.
Let your teachers bring out the best in you.

BE EFFECTIVE
Whatever you set your mind to,
produce the intended outcome.
Burst forth with attractive results.

BE EFFICIENT

Perform and function to the best
and least wasteful manner possible.

BE ELASTIC

Be capable of returning to your original self
after being stretched, stressed,
and bent out of shape.
Have a springy mental and physical constitution.

BE ELATED

Be very happy and proud.
Find a joyous peace of mind
with living in naturally high spirits.

BE ELEGANT

Be pleasingly superior in quality and kind.
Also, be gracefully refined and dignified
as to your tastes, habits, and personal style.

BE ELIGIBLE

Be fit and proper to be chosen.
Be available and worthy of choice.

BE ELOQUENT

Exercise the power
of fluent, forceful, and appropriate speech.

BE EMANCIPATED

Be freed from bondage,
or anything that would constrict
your free movement.
Be unconstrained
by custom, tradition, or superstition.

BE EMPATHETIC

Be able to identify with
the feelings, thoughts, and attitudes of others.
Your ability
to sense the arena of life you are in
will reveal many treasures.

BE ENCHANTING
Find delight within yourself.
Keep focused on how things can be
and instill these possibilities in others
by example.

BE ENCOURAGED
Be inspired with courage and confidence.
Be reassured with your own approval
by giving yourself permission.

BE ENDLESS
Enlarge the insight of your involvement in life.
Expand upon your perception of eternity.

BE ENDURING
Your constitution,
that which is the you of you,
is lasting and permanent.
Be patient and allow growth to occur.

BE ENERGETIC

Flip your switch on
and exhibit spark and vitality
with a childlike enthusiasm.

BE ENERGIZED

Be aroused into activity,
operating with the optimum.
Be excited!

BE ENGAGING

Have a winning smile
and a pleasing influence on others.

BE ENHANCING

Leave a place better than you found it.
Nurture your life with care
and edify your self-image
with attractive elements of decoration.

BE ENJOYABLE
As you are likeable and loveable, be delightful.
Have the capacity to express
and allow joy.

BE ENLIGHTENED
Possess
intellectual and spiritual insight
appropriate to the here and now.

BE ENRAPTURED
Be moved to rapture;
delighted beyond measure.
Get caught up
in the rhapsody of life.

BE ENRICHED
Upgrade your mental outlook
by assimilating the ingredients
of concepts you find valuable.

BE ENTERPRISING

Acquire initiative,
ingenuity,
and energy.
Find a need and fill it.

BE ENTERTAINING

Hold the attention of that which is agreeable,
with that which is amusing.
Know how to treat your guests
as you would want to be treated.

BE ENTHUSIASTIC

Breathe life into your existence
and let your purpose explode.

BE ENTREPRENEURIAL

As you want something done right,
do it yourself.

BE EQUIPPED

You were born equipped with many features:
Your body, your brain, your talents.
Use them.

BE ESSENTIAL

Essence,
in the highest sense of the word,
is the unaltered nature of a thought or thing.
Your "inmost substance"
comes from a state of bliss.
Explore yours.

BE ESTIMABLE

Be worthy of esteem.
Feel good about yourself,
in who, how, and what you're being.

BE ETERNAL

There is a part of you which lasts forever.
You are part of a ceaseless,
endless,
immutable,
eternity.

BE EVEN-TEMPERED

Be relatively calm
when you negotiate your direction
in day-to-day affairs.
Choose to remain unruffled
and maintain a cool-headed composure.

BE EVOLVING

Unfold over time.
Become more of who you are
by blending your possibilities into actualities
in the process of becoming
a new creation.

BE EXCELLENT

Possess superior merit
and be remarkably good.
Be instilled with outstanding qualities
and matchless integrity.

BE EXCEPTIONAL

Be more
than what you would be if you didn't care,
and more
than what you would be if you didn't try.

BE EXCITED

Be aroused and stirred in your emotions
by feeling supreme delight in your activities.
Hope for success.

BE EXHILARATING

Invigorate and stimulate pleasant,
merry laughter,
with good cheer and enthusiasm.

BE EXPEDIENT

Do what it takes to get the job done,
without dragging your feet,
and without destroying or injuring
anyone or anything in the process.

BE EXPERIENCED

Claim your experiences
as your intellectual and emotional property.
Become wise and skillful
in your particular field.

BE EXPERT

Acquire special skills and knowledge
through practice and performance.
Only then can your work become play.
Become the connoisseur and specialist
you dream of becoming.

BE EXPLORING

Look closely;
be curious;
scrutinize;
and examine all that surrounds you in life.

BE EXPRESSIVE

Feel your thoughts
as you speak and write.
Enhance the effects of being heard
with appropriate manners and gestures.
Let your hands and eyes convey the emphasis.

BE EXQUISITE

Your intrinsic beauty and charm
portray an extraordinarily fine
and appealing sense of excellence.
Be the original you are.

BE EXTRAORDINARY
Be exceptional in character,
and signify the remarkable.

BE EXTRICATING
Free yourself from difficult situations.
Disengage from adversity.

BE EXUBERANT
Be extremely joyful and vigorous
while abounding in profuse and luxuriant
growth.

F

BE FABULOUS

Be exceptionally good and unusual.
Familiarize yourself with being marvelous,
and recognize it when it happens for you.
Blossom and be the incredible person
you see you are.

∽

BE FAIR

Play the game I Win—You Win.
Discover what it's like
to be free from bias, dishonesty, and injustice.
Think before you act.

∽

BE FAITHFUL

Be reliable, trustworthy, and believable
in order to know the deep satisfaction
of allegiance and affection.
Be true to your words
and keep your promises.

65

BE FAMILY

Recognize the brotherhood of Men
and the sisterhood of Women.
Participate in this family as the Child you are.
And be thankful to and for
the Father and Mother of us all.

BE FEARLESS

Beckon that which is bold and brave within you.
Reckon with that which you fear.
Draw from the part of you which knows no fear.
Be the Champion.

BE FEELING

Become acquainted
with the nonthinking part of you.
Know your heart.
Give yourself permission
for a capacity of emotions,
especially for compassion.

BE FELICITOUS
Remember that you have a special ability
to be the best you,
and you are well-suited for the occasion.

BE FESTIVE
When it's time to party,
contribute to the joy of celebration.
Dance and be happy.

BE FINDING
Your effort to discover
allows you to obtain.
Permit yourself to put forth the effort.

BE FINE
Be very well
and in an excellent manner.
Emboss your signature of approval
on the fabric of today.

BE FIT

Provide for good physical and mental
conditioning.
Be worthy and deserving.

BE FLEXIBLE

Be capable of being bent.
Be pliable and willing to yield.

BE FLUENT

Practice and learn to speak and write clearly.
Know the patterns of language
and the effects of emotions.
Train your mind to experience communication
with all people in your life.

BE FOCUSED

Adjust whatever is necessary
to become more clear and sharply defined.
Your thinking, seeing, feeling, speaking,
and general being
deserve to be managed with clarity.

BE FOREVER

Who you are and what you do
will in some way live on into eternity.
Think, plan, and decide accordingly.

BE FORGIVEN

Cease feeling resentment against yourself.
Accept pardon
and continue to do that which is right and good.

BE FORTUNATE

Acknowledge each good result,
small and large,
so that you may continue to prosper
from uncertain and unexpected sources.

BE FREE

Enjoy your personal rights and liberty,
and respect that for others.

BE FRESH

Approach each moment as the first,
for each moment has never happened before.
Reflect the brightness of light
rather than cloudiness.
Let the eternal springtime of love
accompany you
through the seasons of your life.

BE FRIENDLY

In order to have friends, be one.
Nurture bonds of affiliation with love and care.
Send or leave notes of cheer and good will
so people can know
that you're thinking well of them.
Invite companions to participate
in your Odyssey of Life
by sharing significant experiences, hardships,
and insights.

BE FRUITFUL

Allow yourself to be productive and useful.
Enjoy bearing the fruits of your labor.
Yield an abundance of truth, beauty,
and goodness.

BE FULFILLED

Notice beauty and value in small things
as well as large.
Embrace the people in your life with satisfaction
and hold dear your achievements.

BE FUN

Provide enjoyment and happiness
at work and play.
Nourish your spirit
with a sense of true pleasure.
Frolic in the high spirits of freedom.

G

BE GAINING

Increase improvement in yourself.
Gather momentum for coming closer
to your goals.
The results of your endeavors are your rewards.

BE GALLANT

Be elegant with your politeness and attention.
Free your high-spirited nature to exist.
Rise to the challenge of being noble.

BE GENEROUS

Be free
from meanness or smallness
of mind or character.
Be liberal
in the giving of your time, talents, and energy.

BE GENIUS

Listen to your guardian spirit
through your heart and mind.
Know your own thoughts.
See your own visions.

∽

BE GENTLE

Be kind and amiable.
Develop that which is mild,
not severe, rough, or violent.
Ingeniously turn fighting into friendship.

∽

BE GENUINE

Proceed as from the original stock,
the original thought.
Free yourself from pretense and deceit.
Embrace the authentic you.

BE GLAD

Attend your presence with all things positive.
For everything bad there is something else good.
Seek the light of happiness
to dissolve the shadows of sadness.

BE GLOBAL

Set the parameters of your perceptions
to include the whole world.

BE GLOWING

Display the radiance of health,
and let the rich colors of life
show in your skin, your eyes, and in your smile.

BE GOOD

Within the genuine there is excellence.
Choose honor and worthiness.
Strive for kindness and benevolence.

BE GOOD-WILLED
Be of a cheerful and friendly disposition.
Be predisposed
toward that which is enheartening for everyone.

BE GRACEFUL
Seek elegance and beauty
in form, manner, movement, and speech.

BE GRACIOUS
Show favor, tolerance, and courtesy to others.
Be characterized by good taste.

BE GRATEFUL
Warmly and deeply appreciate
the mercy and benefits you receive.
Express your gratitude.

BE GRATUITOUS
Give
without the thought or expectation of return.

BE GREAT
Be of high principle.
Darkness cannot exist in the presence of light.

BE GREGARIOUS
Enjoy meeting new people
and developing your social network.
Hang out with your friends
and chew the fat with your family.

BE GROWING
By degree, come to be.
Assimilate the nutrients
of love, life, light, and liberty.

BE GUTSY

Exercise your nerve and courage.
Stand up for what you believe.

H

BE HANDY
Be skillful with your hands.
Get involved and maintain your environment.
Fix things with your ingenuity.

∽

BE HAPPY
Contemplate thoughts
which are delightful and pleasing.
Be apt for joy and felicitous
through your actions, utterances, and ideas.
Have a propensity to laugh.

∽

BE HARMONIOUS
Help to form a pleasingly consistent wholeness.
Be congruent and agreeable
in your thoughts, feelings, and actions,
and create euphony within and around you.

BE HEALTHY

Possess and enjoy good health
and a sound, vigorous mentality.
Preserve a wholesome presence
with beneficial attitudes.

BE HEARTWARMING

Be gratifying, rewarding, and satisfying.
Tenderly move the emotions.

BE HEARTY

Be warm-hearted, affectionate, cordial,
and jovial.
Express heartfelt, genuine, and sincere
enthusiasm.
Be abundant, substantial, and nourishing.

BE HELPFUL

Be of service
and quick to give assistance.

BE HERE

Be in this place
and at this time,
physically, mentally, and emotionally.

BE HOME

Abide at ease
in the place where your heart can feel deeply
and your mind can be clear.
Enjoy your privacy.

BE HONEST

Signify the honorable
in principles, intentions, and actions.
Be genuine and unadulterated.
Show fairness and sincerity.

BE HONORABLE

Exist in accordance with principles of honor.
Be worthy of high respect.
Qualify your character with credibility.

BE HOPEFUL

Hope is the life blood of success,
a close relative of faith.
It is what you believe in but have not yet seen.

BE HOSPITABLE

Receive and treat guests and strangers
as you would want to be received and treated,
warmly and generously.

BE HUMANE

Act as a benefactor
for those less fortunate than you.
Be merciful, compassionate,
and gracious in empathy.
Strive to encourage spiritual evolution
with regard for all living creatures.

BE HUMBLE

Allow neither praise nor slander to influence you.
Know who you are,
but let others discover it for themselves.

BE HUMOROUS

Have a sense of humor.
Do not take yourself so seriously
that you cannot appreciate the music
of laughter.

I

BE IDEALISTIC
Pursue the concepts and things
which you believe ought to be.
Do not be trapped by what seems to be.

BE ILLUMINATED
Be enlightened
and radiate the light of your understanding
with clarity.

BE IMAGINATIVE
Foster your creativity
and exploit your imagination.
Investigate ways to free it.

BE IMPORTANT
Direct the intentions of your life with purpose
and avoid dwelling on the trivial.

BE IMPROVING

Bring yourself, your thoughts,
and everything around you,
into ever more excellent conditions.

BE IMPROVISING

Be spontaneous.
Act without previous preparation,
trusting your wisdom, instincts, and insights.

BE INCOMPARABLE

Refrain from contrasting yourself with others.
The measure of all things is relative.
Possess your own set of standards.

BE INCREDIBLE

Inspire others with your life.
Define your own path
and do what you dream of doing.

BE INDEPENDENT

Establish your own life and liberty.
Rely on your own abilities and resources.

BE INFINITE

Extend the boundaries of your vision
into territories not yet defined.

BE INFORMATIVE

When information is requested of you,
give it willingly.
Support the dissemination of information.

BE INGENIOUS

Look at things in a way no one else does.
Your clever solutions and resourceful approaches
make you a valuable associate.

BE INQUISITIVE
Knowledge is asking and finding.
Wisdom is willingness and discovery.
Experience is involvement and refinement.

BE INSPIRED
Be imbued with the spirit to do special things.
Act from the viewpoint
that a superior intelligence
is influencing and empowering you
and your purpose.

BE INSTRUMENTAL
Be helpful and useful.
Apply yourself with vision and clarity.

BE INTELLIGENT
Have a quickness of understanding,
displaying sound thought
and well-founded reasoning.

BE INTELLIGIBLE

Be capable of being understood.
Be as clear as possible in your speech
and writing.

BE INTERCESSIVE

In times of difficulty and trouble,
act on the behalf of
family, friends, and associates
to help smooth things out.
Build a spirit of teamwork.

BE INTERESTED

Participate in activities
which have the power to engage your curiosity.
Display an attentiveness
for what you desire.

BE INTIMATE

Intimacy is the closeness of love
where the innermost affairs of the heart
are shared.
Produce a favorable environment
for sharing essential feelings and poetic beauty
in your friend-ships.

BE INTUITIVE

Let your keen insight
provide a quick process
for discerning truth, fact, and knowledge.
Use your intuition.

BE INVALUABLE

You are of inestimable worth
and therefore priceless.
The splendor of your being
is beyond appraisable value.

BE INVENTIVE

Create new products, ideas, and techniques
when you envision better methods and ideals.
Act on your instincts
to improve conditions
and have a propensity to be inspired.

∽

BE INVITING

Offer friendship
which is both attractive and alluring.
Request the presence and participation
of your family, friends, and associates
with a kind, courteous, and complementary
atmosphere.

∽

BE INVOLVED

Engage your interests and emotions
with purposes you adopt.
Get into the thick of it and contribute.
Participate.

J

BE JAZZED
Choose to be alive and spirited.
Approach life with an inclination for the off-beat
and emulate the privilege to improvise.

BE JOYFUL
Be full of delight
and express a thrill for life.
Spread happiness
and be of good cheer.

BE JUDGELESS
Suspend closure of your mind.
Avoid forming inflexible judgments
and unalterable opinions.

BE JUDICIOUS

Exercise your faculty of good judgment.
Choose to be wise, sensible, and well-advised.

K

BE KEEN

Be highly sensitive and perceptive.
Be enthusiastic in your endeavors
and ardent in your dreams.

∽

BE KIND

Preoccupy yourself with a loving disposition.
Choose to be gracious and giving.

∽

BE KISSABLE

Choose to be physically, mentally, and spiritually
attractive and beautiful.

∽

BE KNOWING

Embrace what you know,
and enjoy the insight of this awareness.
Give yourself credit for your experiences.
Let wisdom guide your intuition.

L

BE LAWFUL

You will either be bound by the law
or set free by the law.
It's up to you whether you see bars or stars.
Learn to live within the parameters of love
and expose the social structure of order
to justice.

∽

BE LEADING

Be a leader
with no one following you.
Choose to prompt your own thinking
and actions.
Deduce your own set of values.

∽

BE LEARNING

Acquire skills
through study, instruction, and experience.
Establish your habits and mannerisms
through exposure to examples.

BE LEGIBLE
Be discernible.
Let your writings be capable
of being easily
read and understood.
Send memorable memos
and leave noteworthy messages.

BE LEISURELY
Allow yourself
to include the peace of relaxation
in your routine of activities.

BE LIBERAL
Favor progress and reform.
Permit freedom of action for yourself first.
Remain open-minded
and abide by your generous, personal beliefs
and willingness to give.

BE LIBERATED
Be set free from bondage and fear
by releasing their grip on your attention.
Prevail in a state of freedom.

BE LIEVE
Lieve is a word which means gladly and
willingly desirous.
It also means dear one, beloved, and treasured.
You are.

BE LIGHT
Let your mental and spiritual illumination
be made visible to others through your actions.
Display a cheerful and sunny disposition.

BE LIGHT-HEARTED
Be buoyant, upbeat, and optimistic.
Let your uplifting confidence
permeate your surroundings.

BE LISTENING

Pay attention to others
when conversing with them.
Take note of what they are saying,
and, especially, to what they are not saying.
Then ask if your perceptions are correct.

BE LITERATE

Be able to read and write.
Join the world of information
and enjoy it.

BE LOVE

You are the subject and object
of warm, personal attachment
and deep affection
by your family and friends.
Be the miracle you are.

BE LOVING
Show affection and love.
Express your affinities and good feelings
as often as you like.

BE LOVELY
Be charming and exquisitely beautiful.
Appeal to the heart as well as to the eye.

BE LUMINOUS
Be an inspiration for others.
Allow the truth
to shine through you
clearly and lucidly.

BE LUXURIANT
Let your life be
as abundant in growth as vegetation,
producing fruits of truth, beauty, and goodness.
Be richly inexhaustible
in the garden of your character.

M

BE MAGICAL
Use creatively diverse techniques
to produce effects
which render the ordinary
amazing and remarkable.
Enhance your life with the unique and unusu

BE MAGNANIMOUS
Be generous in forgiving insults and injury.
Be free from petty resentfulness.
and maintain a high-minded nobility.

BE MAGNETIC
Display a strong, attractive power, and charm
Position all of your positive thoughts and
feelings
up front.
Repel negative forces
with an optimistic mastery.

BE MAGNIFICENT

There is nothing so great that you cannot
become it.
There is nothing so grand that you cannot
attain it.

BE MAINTAINING

Do what is necessary
to continue being the way you want to be.
Affirm the postures you choose to take.
Conduct your existence with a watchful eye
and manual dexterity,
enjoying the many benefits
of a healthy approach to life.

BE MANAGING

Bring order and harmony into your life.
Contrive to organize your success,
overcoming
depression, hardships, difficulties,
and disappointments.

BE MARVELOUS

Choose to be superb and excellent
in all that you do,
and all that you are.
Arouse wonder and astonishment
as you explore and discover
the world within you and around you.

BE MASTERFUL

Display skill with your talents
and wisdom from your experience.
Be unconsciously competent.

BE MATURING

Allow yourself to undergo the development
of your body, mind, and spirit.
Feel and consider the natural growth
inherent in living day-by-day.
Become ever more aware of the response-ability
of your mind.

BE MEDITATIVE
Take time to contemplate
issues which matter most to you.
Make your decisions with a clear mind.
Shift gears by going through neutral first.

BE MEEK
Be gentle and kind.
Represent
goodness and humility
through your words and actions.

BE MERRY
Be filled with cheerfulness and gaiety,
joyous in your disposition.
Let your spirit enjoy mirth on earth.

BE MIGHTY

Be exceptional in your strength of character.
Uphold truths and principles which act
to promote life, liberty,
and the pursuit of happiness.

BE MINGLING

Participate in the company you keep.
Associate with those you love
and have yet to love.

BE MIRACLE-MINDED

Believe in the miracles that take place
in this world.
Appreciate being part of events
in the physical world
which surpass all known human wherewithal.
Be open to what you do not understand.

BE MIRTHFUL

Feel exuberantly happy
and give audible expression.
Let laughter heal.

BE MODELING
You are being imitated
by those whose lives you touch.
Exemplify that which is desirable.

BE MODEST
Be free from ostentation
or showy extravagance.
Temper your appetite with moderation.

BE MORAL
Be concerned with right conduct and principles.
Do no thing least of all you love it.
Conform to principle
rather than to law or custom.
Listen to your heart.

BE MOTIVATED
Tempt yourself to act
by imagining how you will feel
having accomplished your goals.
Create your own incentives.

BE MUNIFICENT

Display great generosity.
You may not be able to outgive the universe,
but you can try.

BE MUSICAL

There is within you
a melodious, harmonious, and rhythmic spirit.
Let it be uninhibited.
Respond with it.

BE MUTUAL

See eye to eye with others.
Make your relationship with others reciprocal.

BE MYSELF

Above all else, be who you are.
Get acquainted with all of yourself.
Discern the "I Am."

N

BE NATURAL
Exist
in accordance with patterns and principles
of nature.
Embrace
the intrinsic value and constitution
you were born with.
Your essence
contains the actual and the potential.

∽

BE NEAT
Place your world
in a pleasingly orderly condition.
Be admirably fastidious and attractively nice.

∽

BE NECESSARY
Be essential,
indispensable,
and requisite.

BE NEGOTIATING

Everything is made of mind
and its modifications.
Come to equal terms with others
and maneuver compensation
to gain equally with what is given.

BE NEIGHBORLY

Show qualities befitting a neighbor.
Overcome the tendency for isolation in life
by being friendly, helpful, and respectful.
Encourage a sense of community.
Promote friendship.

BE NETWORKING

Establish a social and empathetic relationship
with others.
Initiate and integrate
associations and connections.

BE NEW

Every moment is unique.
It has never been before.
It will never be again.
Each minute is appearing for the very first time.
Welcome it, praise it, and make it count.

BE NICE

Be amiably pleasant, kind, desirable,
and delightful.
Package and promote the best of yourself.

BE NIFTY

Be clever and stylish.
Be known
for expressing your own unique place
in the universe.

BE NOBLE

Constitute in your personality
that which is of admirably high quality.
Discern what is good and right.
Follow your path
and it will lead you to a high regard for life.

BE NOURISHING

Supplement the body with good food,
and the mind with good thought.
Strengthen
the truth, beauty, and richness
within you
by endorsing that which is worthy of you.

BE NOVEL

Choose to be relatively new
and of a different kind.
Remain fresh and original.

BE NURTURING

Promote development
and encourage growth,
of body, mind, and spirit.
Offer a helping hand
by sharing your understanding and knowledge.

O

BE OBSERVANT

Be quick to notice and perceive.
Pay attention to your surroundings,
and keep your eyes on the road.

BE OCCUPIED

Engage your attention wisely.
Apply your mind
to the tasks you have set
for yourself.

BE OPEN-HEARTED

Be unreserved, candid, and frank.
Keep your love available
with your personality, individuality,
and character
in a seemingly impersonal world.

BE OPEN-MINDED
Recognize
how the processes of thinking
and the contents of thought
flow wonderfully
when you are receptive
to new ideas and arguments.
Be unprejudiced in your perceptions.

BE OPTIMAL
Be the best and most desirable you can be.
Choose to orient yourself toward tasty results
and rewards that are well worth it.

BE OPTIMISTIC
Possess a propensity
for taking a favorable view.
Reflect on your possibilities with hope.
Be convinced.

BE ORGANIZED
Put yourself into a state
of physical and mental competence and order,
prepared to perform the task at hand.
Know where things are.

BE ORIGINAL
Belong to the beginning thought.
Connect yourself to that which is inventive
and creative.
Allow this source to flow through you,
and sustain a fresh channel for new ideas.

BE OUTSTANDING
Seek to be skillful with your talents.
Earn the prominence that will make you
pleasantly conspicuous.

BE OVERCOMING
Prevail.
The future can be better because of you.

BE OWNING

Recognize that you have legitimate claim,
authority, power, and dominion over your life.
Take charge and care for it.

P

BE PARENTAL
Be an ideal guardian.
Bestow on those in your custody
the love and skills they will need to learn
to support themselves
and eventually parent others.

BE PARTICIPATING
Take part in activities
with your friends, associates, and family.
Share with them
and enable them to share with you.

BE PARTYING
Know how to party.
Enjoy the conversation, refreshments,
entertainment,
and laughter.
Take time to be free of responsibilities
and burdens.

BE PASSIONATE
Embrace the strong feelings
and intense emotions
that are sparked within your soul
and spread like wild fire throughout your body.
Breathe deeply and experience your ardent fever.

BE PATIENT
Be diligent in details which ensure success.
Persevere through pain and discomfort,
without complaint and anger.

BE PEACEFUL

Be inclined to avoid strife and dissension.
Proceed from a state of mind which is tranquil,
always seeking the path
which promotes harmony.

BE PERCEPTIVE

Use your second sight.
See without your eyes and hear the inner voice.
Let insight and understanding guide you.

BE PERFECTIVE

Strive to make things perfect.
Apply yourself always toward improvement
and endeavor to be replete
within your sphere of existence.

BE PERFORMING

Know the point
when practicing must turn into performance.
Execute the skills you have perfected.
Remember your lessons well.

BE PERSEVERING

Persist in what you choose to undertake.
Maintain a sense of purpose
and sustain your dreams;
they are the guiding light to your future.

BE PERSONABLE

Give others the gift of your warm ambiance
and friendly charisma.
Be likeable and outgoing.

BE PERSUASIVE

Win over others to your efforts.
Let your enthusiasm
be the key that opens the doors.

BE PHENOMENAL

Choose to feel wonderful,
and see your life as extraordinary.
When you can truly please yourself
your sincerity will be genuinely unprecedented.

BE PHILOSOPHICAL
Become well-versed in truths and principles.
Know and understand
the world in which you live.

BE PHYSICAL
Give your body the activity it needs
to breathe and support
the life you choose to embrace.
Let your actions
provide you with tangible experience.

BE PIONEERING
Be the first,
be adventurous,
and be original in your pursuits.
Pave the way for others.

BE PLANNING

Mentally project
the proceedings of your daily tasks and efforts.
Predesign your course of action
for effective results.

BE PLAYFUL

Be able to take delight in pleasurable activities.
Release your frolicsome nature
and let it bring you happiness.
Recapture the uninhibited part of your childhood
and get back in touch with your core being.
Utilize this energy to balance your life.

BE PLEASANT

Be agreeable and enjoyable.
Cultivate an amiable personality,
polite manners, and a social disposition.

BE PLENTIFUL

Recognize and seize that great river of thought
which flows within you
yearning to yield abundant fruit.

BE POETIC

Endow your thoughts and expressions
with a creative flair.
Express from your heart
the beauty and depth felt
when to the essence of life you commit yourself.

BE POISED

Maintain a state of balance and equilibrium.
Let your posture be composed with dignity.
Carry your "Self" with assurance and confidence.

BE POLISHED

Allow the rough edges of your personality
to be smoothed through exposure to time
and experience.

BE POLITE

Show good manners toward others.
Choose for your behavior, speech,
and movement
to be uncommonly courteous.

BE POSITIVE

Proceed in a direction
which is potentially most beneficial
and progressive.
Emphasize that which is laudable, hopeful,
and desirable.
Express an unconditional confidence.

BE POSTURED

Orchestrate your mental and spiritual attitudes.
Let your body reflect a healthy self-esteem.
Position your mind for success.
Stand tall.

BE POWERFUL

Within the constitution of your nature
remember your personal history
of strength and endurance.
Command the attention
of the people and
resources needed
by building on all that has brought you
to this moment.

BE PRACTICING

Habit can be your best friend.
Habit is why you are the way you are.
Become proficient
with using this natural resource,
but do not let it blind or numb you into a rut.

BE PRAISING

Remember to voice your admiration for others
just as you enjoy their approval.

BE PRECIOUS

Esteem yourself to be priceless
and of great value.
Be dear and be loved.

∽

BE PREPARED

Put thoughts and matters into proper condition.
Maintain readiness and familiarize yourself
with that which is to be expected
and unexpected.

∽

BE PRESENT

Let all the faculties of your existence function
here and now.
Attend your presence
with all of your sensibilities.

∽

BE PRODUCTIVE

Display powers of performance.
Cause and bring about the results you work for.

BE PROFESSIONAL

Polish yourself into the leader you dream to be.
Maintain an attitude of being the best;
willing to operate
on a level commensurate with your abilities.

BE PROFITABLE

Be beneficial and useful.
Harvest the rewards you have worked for.
Master the science and nature of economics.

BE PROFOUND

Be intellectually penetrating,
pursuing insight with depth of thought and
feeling.
Explore your mind and heart
below the surface of conscious awareness.
Originate from the depths of your being.

BE PROGRESSIVE

Be one who advocates progress
within technology, sociology, and theology.
Be forward thinking
and excited about possibilities.

BE PROLIFIC

Abundant productivity is within your capabilities.
Produce liberally with care and efficiency.

BE PROPORTIONAL

Size is relative;
adjust your perspective
to live in harmony and balance.
Integrate body, mind, and spirit with symmetry.

BE PROSPEROUS

Handle your success, wealth, and welfare
with comfort.
Acknowledge the richness of life
and good fortune you deserve.

BE PROUD
Think well
of the accomplishments and character
of yourself and others.
Recognize quality and promote it.
Be well-pleased.

BE PRUDENT
Be judicious and careful in your affairs.
Provide for the future
by managing resources today.

BE PURE-HEARTED
Choose to expose your innocence
without naiveté.
Be free from malice, treachery, and evil intent.

BE PURPOSEFUL
Acquire a motive.
Determine for yourself what you want
and take the steps to achieve it.

Q

BE QUALITY
Demonstrate the highest character
in both thought and action.
Be conscious of your thinking.
Enjoy the distinction of having attributes
which are great, noble, and excellent.

BE QUESTIONING
Cultivate an alert and curious mind.
Let your intellectual pursuits
help you discover who you are,
why things are the way they are,
and why you are here.

R

BE RADIANT

An ambience of good health
shines ever more brightly
when you top it off with your smile.
Emit rays of hope and joy.

BE RALLYING

Revive your spirit of strength and cause.
Instill your purpose with fresh vigor.
Enlist the support of others.

BE RATIONAL

You are endowed with the faculty of reasoning.
Exercise it.
Show good judgment and "common" sense.

BE READY
Be prepared
and in fit condition
for immediate response and action.
Don't hesitate.
Be willing.

BE REAL
Have an actual,
rather than an imaginary,
existence.
Choose to be genuine and authentic.

BE REALIZED
Begin with you and grow toward your future.
Understand and reach for the reality
you've chosen.

BE REASONABLE

Choose to be agreeable to
and in accordance with
reason, logic, and insight.
Be rational in your understandings
and spice them up with appropriate feelings

BE REASSURED

Choose to be confident.
Assure yourself of this again and again,
until it becomes second nature.

BE REBORN

Renew your existence through growth.
Experience your own personal renaissance,
by letting go of who you think you are
for who you think you can become.

BE RECEIVED

Acquaint yourself with feeling welcomed,
accepted as a guest and member of the family.
Do not shy away from that which is given to you
freely from those who know you.

∽

BE RECEPTIVE

Be open to suggestions and ideas,
able to access knowledge,
and inclined to intelligently admit mistakes
as well as success.

∽

BE RECIPROCAL

Be complementary in your affairs.
Give, perform, and feel in return with others.
Decide upon an equal exchange
in your relationships.
Graduate from the theory of
return-on-investment
to a more supernal concept
of mutually giving without the thought of
return.
Communicate.

BE RECOLLECTING

Recall to mind
those memories which
edify your being.
Learn from the pain and the joy.
Recover knowledge from the past.
Appraise your personal history.

BE RECOMMENDING

Be suggestive of those special things
which can be beneficial to others.
Promote quality and value.

BE RECYCLING

Dedicate yourself to being resourceful.
Join in the art form
of reprocessing raw material.
Be mindful of what is available.

BE REJOICING

Choose to see good.
Celebrate your blessings.
Take delight
in your associations and relationships,
bringing joy
to the lives of others
through your own gladness.

BE RELAXED

Be free from the effects of tension and anxiety.
Learn to let your body and mind
let go of
the demands placed on them.
Re-energize yourself through rest.

BE RELIABLE

Choose to be trustworthy
and predispose your character to be honest.
Do what you say you're going to do.

BE RELIEVED

Choose to be free from anxiety, fear, and pain.
Enjoy the lightness of releasing them.

BE RELISHING

Take pleasure in your thoughts and habits.
Thrive on your increasing awareness of pleasure
Find satisfaction within yourself.

BE REMARKABLE

Strive to be worthy of notice.
Let your actions and appearance
speak well of you,
and others will speak in like-kind.

BE REPLETE

Respond to the source of life
within your range of existence,
and let the blueprint for your attainment
and completion
be drawn out by your faith and willingness.

BE RESILIENT

Choose to spring back
from exhaustion, illness, depression,
and adversity.
Resume your life with wholeness and purpose.

BE RESOLUTE

Make up your mind
to make your dreams and visions come true.
Be firmly resolved and determined.

BE RESOURCEFUL

Deal skillfully and promptly with new situations.
Use what is available to you
to overcome difficulties and solve problems.

BE RESPECTABLE

Promote a reputation
worthy of respect and esteem.
Choose to be of value.

BE RESPONSIBLE

Be directly answerable
for the effects of your thoughts and actions.
Accept the consequences
for what you cause to bring about.
Take ownership of your life.

BE RESPONSIVE

Allow yourself to hear, to feel, to think,
and to see.
Be ready to answer
and reply within the spirit intended.

BE REWARDING

Remember to recognize results
and acknowledge them,
whether they belong to you or someone else.

BE RHAPSODIC

Experience the nature
of outrageously enthusiastic
and ecstatic states of spirit.
Let your mind be transported
by supernal concepts.

BE RHYTHMIC

Hear the music of your soul.
Develop your sense of natural movement
and timing
of both body and mind.

BE RICH

Acknowledge your possessions,
and avoid having them possess you.
Be generous in your abundance.

BE RIGHT

Live in accordance with
whatsoever is good, proper, just, and great.
Define and choose this for yourself.
Let insight be your escort.

BE ROMANTIC

Subordinate form to content
and encourage freedom of the heart.
Express your emotions and celebrate nature.
Partake in the adventure of love
and the ideals of passion.

S

BE SAGACIOUS

Develop an acute mental discernment
and show a keen practical sense for your life.
Show respect for the wisdom of others,
for therein lies your own.

∽

BE SANITARY

Be predisposed toward cleanliness.
Take precautions against disease,
and favor health.
Be free from the bacteria
of destructive thinking.

∽

BE SAVING

Be thrifty and economical.
Preserve your compensations
and your treasures,
to one day redeem your future.

BE SAVORY
Create an ambience about you
which is pleasing, attractive, and agreeable.

BE SAVVY
Sharpen your perception and intuition.
Be a step ahead.
Know a lot but understand more.

BE SCINTILLATING
Let your mind captivate others
with its brilliance.
Show your smile
and ignite sparks of life in your eyes.

BE SECURE
Choose to be free in your choices.
Believe in yourself and be confident
of your survival.
Do whatever it takes to be safe,
and then enjoy your privacy.

BE SEDULOUS

Be diligent in your application of attention.
Persevere in the pursuit of your dreams
and maintain your goal setting.

BE SEEING

Open your inner and outer eyes.
Look around and watch,
then perceive
in order to understand clearly.

BE SEEKING

It is the question that leads to answers.
Join the cycle of asking, searching, and finding.
Make requests.

BE SELF-ASSURED

Trust in yourself
and develop an internal dialogue of confidence.
Be familiar with faith, reliance,
and positive certainty.

BE SELF-COMMANDED
Choose to be self-collected and self-controlled.
Give yourself permission
to be in charge of your life.
Don't give up.

BE SELF-CONTROLLED
Exercise appropriate hold
over your actions, feelings, and emotions,
recognizing, too,
when it is most appropriate to let go.

BE SELF-ESTEEMED
Create personal value,
and respect that only you can say
who and how you are.

BE SENSITIVE
Open your heart
and be in tune with other people.
Treat their feelings
with the same care and respect
as you do your own.

BE SENSUOUS
Be acquainted with your senses.
Be acquainted with other's senses.
Enjoy those that are shared.

BE SERENDIPITOUS
Seek that which is important to you
to allow for synchronous discoveries.
Enjoy making the connection.

BE SERENE

Remain unruffled
in the midst of the winds of human drama.
Take counsel in the peaceful and the tranquil.
Be fair and clear.

BE SEXY

Be exciting and enticing,
enlisting all the depths of your person.
Reveal the essence of your gender.
Communicate your capacity for pleasure.

BE SHARP

Be mentally acute, alert, and vigilant.
The steering wheel is in your hands.
Be a responsible driver.

BE SHARING

Pool your resources with others.
Participate for better and worse,
in sickness and in health.

BE SIGNIFICANT

Let the purpose of your life
contain a remarkable kind of importance.
Who you believe you are
has consequences beyond belief.

BE SINCERE

Be genuine,
free from deceit and hypocrisy,
and enjoy the distinction of a meaningful life.

BE SINGLEMINDED

Be dedicated to your vision.
Remain steadfast upon your journey.
Peace of mind will guide you in your quest.

BE SKILLFUL

Apply your abilities to do things.
Cultivate your talents to become expert.
Training, talent, and experience
combine for success.

BE SOCIABLE

Be inclined to associate with others;
predisposed toward friendship.
Between us there is so much to learn and enjo

BE SONGFUL

Cultivate the warehouse of songs within you
and let the tunes of your heart
fill your life.

BE SOOTHING

Be a source of solace for others.
Calm churning feelings with patience, care,
and understanding.

BE SOULFUL

Know your soul;
touch all the seeds of truth, beauty,
and goodness.
Draw upon the deepest parts of yourself,
and express the dance, art, music, and literatu
that dwell within.

BE SPECIAL

Let yourself be distinct.
Let yourself stand apart from others.
The price of blending in is higher
than being unique.

BE SPECTACULAR

First impressions have a lasting effect.
Display yourself dramatically
and let your adventures be daring and thrilling.

BE SPIRITUAL

Be motivated by love,
activated by unselfish participation,
and dominated toward the ideals of truth,
beauty,
and goodness.
Awaken to the needs of others
and be of assistance.

BE SPLENDID

Go beyond the ordinary.
Let your qualities be magnificent
and strikingly admirable.

BE SPONTANEOUS

Have a propensity to express yourself
in the moment.
Say what needs to be said,
when it needs to be said.
Go forward in your movement.

BE STELLULAR

Sparkle like a star
in your particular field of endeavor.
Dwell on aspects and issues
that have far-reaching effects.
Shine within the bubble of our universe.

BE STEWARDING

Manage to take care of your own.
Hold your children's future in trust.
Honor that which has already been
accomplished.

∽

BE STILL

Learn the flow of time.
Grow past survival into Being.
Keep on keeping on.

∽

BE STIMULATING

Rouse others to action with encouragement.
Incite effort
with your own participation.

∽

BE STRIVING

Exert yourself vigorously
and apply yourself repetitively
toward attaining your goals
until you do.

BE STRONG
Deliver results
through use of great physical, mental,
and mechanical power.
Apply your robust presence
with both seen and unseen forces.

BE STUDIOUS
Investigate the nature and knowledge
of your interests.
Examine and scrutinize all aspects.
Be zealous in your analysis.

BE STUPENDOUS
Undertake that
which has never been done before.
Accomplish what only dreamers can see.
Be marvelous.

BE STURDY

Have solid foundations and be strongly built.
Withstand the weather of daily life
and the passing of generations
by having a sincere attitude
and a hearty appetite.

BE SUBJECTIVE

Engage your personality
before you employ your impersonality.
Objectivity is form, subjectivity is content.
Glue your relationships together
with a healthy balance of both.

BE SUBLIME

Impress the mind with a sense of grandeur,
inspiring awe in thought, language,
and presence.
Elevate your thinking
toward a higher, nobler, and purer sense of life.

BE SUBLIMINAL

Employ messages which exist below the threshold
of consciousness.
Trust body language and facial expressions.

BE SUBSTANTIAL

Let there be merit in your accomplishments,
and let the effects of your life reveal true value
Weigh meanings in terms of what you know
and understand.

BE SUBTLE

Be clever, skillful, and ingenious.
Deliver results which require mental acuteness
and discerning penetration.

BE SUCCESSFUL

Acknowledge the accomplishments
you've already achieved.
Attend your life
with an appreciation for attainment.
Enjoy your rewards, prizes, honors,
and compliments.

BE SUCCULENT

Be rich in desirable qualities.
Afford delight to the sensibilities of others.
Let your fruitfulness be full of juice.

BE SUMPTUOUS

Permeate your personality and life-style
with that which is luxuriously fine, splendid,
and superb.

BE SUNNY

Applaud that which is cheerful and joyous.
Reflect the light of a happy outlook.

BE SUPERB

Be grand in your countenance
and excellent in the qualities you adhere to.

BE SUPERNAL

Increase your capacity
to behold heavenly precepts and contents.
Let the celestial light of love and understanding
shine in your eyes and in your mind.

BE SUPPORTABLE

Be capable
of being maintained with a foundation.
Create a livelihood which is endurable.
Allow others to assist you when needed.

BE SUPPORTIVE

Assist others, giving aid as part of a team.
Supply a loving attitude.

BE SUPREME

Personalize the truth of intellectual meaning,
the beauty of physical harmony,
and the goodness of spiritual value.

BE SURE

Let your mind attain a level of certainty
which is free from doubt
as to your reliability, character, and actions.
Be confident with what you expect.

BE SUSTAINED

Persist with confidence along your path.
Believe in your strength and abilities.

BE SWEET

Be pleasing and agreeable.
Have a pleasant disposition
and a fragrant personality.

BE SWELL

Be a buddy to someone.
Let your influence be timely and vital.

BE SWIFT

Be capable of moving with great speed.
Respond quickly to opportunities
and move with them.
Be happening.

BE SYMPATHETIC

Be compassionate
and look upon others with favor.
Have mutual relationships
which exhibit special affinities.

BE SYNERGISTIC

Let one plus one equal three.
Work together
and sanction a sum greater than its parts.
A three-sided structure
is the strongest foundation in our universe.

T

BE TACTFUL

Manifest a keen sense
of what to do or say to avoid offending others.
Be diplomatic.

✍

BE TALENTED

Unfold your capacity
for expression, achievement, and success.
Acknowledge your special abilities
and amplify your aptitudes.

✍

BE TEACHING

Impart your knowledge,
and educate others
in the skills you've mastered.

BE TEACHABLE

Be capable of being taught,
open to instruction.
Increase your net worth
through guidance and training.

BE TEMPERATE

Moderate yourself and your indulgences.
Be self-restrained and not extreme
in your actions, opinions, and statements.

BE TENACIOUS

Hold fast to your beliefs.
Train your mind to be highly retentive.
Keep your identity together
with a sense of purpose.

BE TENDER

Express love and affection.
Be easily moved to empathy and compassion.
Be gentle and sensitive.

BE TERRESTRIAL
Consider yourself at home.
Consider yourself an inhabitant of planet earth.
Let your stay here
be filled with joy, love, and respect.

∽

BE TERRIFIC
Be extraordinarily great, intense, and good.
Esteem yourself with an "eager to be" essence.

∽

BE THANKFUL
Admit your feelings of appreciation
and express your gratitude.
Let it edify your spirit.

BE THINKING

Let the river of thought
fill your mind
and offer a rationale to life.
Be careful in designing ideas with your mind.
Ponder your opinions
and refine your conjectures.

BE THOROUGHGOING

Ride the crest of the wave.
Let yourself experience the fullness of your self.
Carry things out
to their fullest extent in your observation.

BE THOUGHTFUL

Be given toward handling your life
with consideration for others,
as well as for yourself.
Be mindful
of the explosive nature
of your contemplations.
To think is to create.

BE THRIFTY

Participate in a world of economics.
Learn how to manage your personal economy.
Make the most of your money.
Make the most of your energy.

BE THRIVING

Develop a vigorous
and flourishing mode of being.
Go beyond merely existing into a life
vibrating with a spirit of love and appreciation.

BE TIMELESS

Be restricted to no particular time.
Be part of the past as well as the future.

BE TIMELY

Trust your sense of what needs to be, when.
Seize the day and make it yours.

BE TOGETHER

Develop and nurture relationships
which are reciprocal.
Enjoy talking with others
and spend quality time with them.

BE TOLERANT

Have a predisposition toward endurance.
Support others
as you would yourself wish to be supported.
Pardon inconveniences with patience
and understanding.

BE TOUCHING

Be affectionate enough to touch others.
Let there be healing and love in your hands.

BE TOUGH
Be able to withstand hardships.
Be resistant
toward the mental and physical viruses
which are ever present.
Be tenacious.

◌

BE TRANQUIL
Be free from lasting effects
of disturbing emotions.
Be free from the effects of commotion
and tumultuous conditions.
Seek balance.

◌

BE TRANSCENDENTAL
Go beyond the ordinary limits.
Surpass the expected
and clothe yourself with that which you feel
you can become.

BE TREASURED

Regard yourself as highly valued and cherished.
Remember that what you are becoming
is part of a wonderful secret yet to be told.

∽

BE TRIUMPHANT

Rejoice over victory.
Be exultant over the magnificence of success
and justice.
Enjoy the trophy.

∽

BE TRUE

Be faithful to the authentic
in the best and most desirable sense.
Reflect the sincerity of your feelings
and intentions
by allowing yourself to have basis in fact
and action.
Remain loyal to your word.

BE TRUSTWORTHY

Generate belief in you by others
for your dependability and reliability
by creating assurance of this in yourself.

BE TRUTHFUL

Habitually tell the truth.
Permit yourself the privilege and pleasure
of having no lies to hide from.

U

BE UNAFRAID
Fear need not impair you.
Let it bring your attention
to the matter needing your awareness.

BE UNASHAMED
Embarrassment restrains.
Understanding the nature of belittlement
is the key to healing
the hiding and pain caused by shame.
Awkwardness passes only as an event
to be learned from.
It is not a status you acquire.

BE UNBIASED
Position yourself to take a flexible viewpoint
that may be missed
by others involved to one extreme or another.

BE UNCONDITIONAL
Live your life
without endlessly prequalifying
requirements necessary
for wholehearted participation.
Let the sinews of your integrity
support your sincerity.

BE UNDAUNTED
Hold onto your vision
firmly and clearly.
Fuel your imagination
with the inspiration of courage and valor.

BE UNDENIABLE
Attribute to yourself
characteristics which belong to you
through divine inheritance.
Adopt ideals
which are not open to refusal or repulsion.

BE UNDERSTANDING

Demonstrate your ability
to interpret information.
Let your mind be engaged
with reason, common sense, and concepts
which act to scaffold your awareness
and appreciation.

BE UNIQUE

Be incomparable.
Stand alone in your own particular qualities.
Cast your own shadow.
Apply your own distinct characteristics
as to how you are, what you do,
and how you do it.

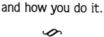

BE UNISONOUS

Exist in a state of alignment with others
sharing viewpoints, feelings, and dreams.

BE UNITED

Experience togetherness;
be with people.
Turn your organization into a living organism.
Act as part of the concert of life.

BE UNIVERSAL

Expand your perception to be all-embracing.
See things
as belonging, affecting, concerning,
and involving everybody.
Grasp the "whole" picture.

BE UNLIMITED

Nothing is beyond you.
Modify your thinking and feeling
to include that which is boundless, infinite,
and vast
within your creativity.
Drink a glass of water
and touch the endless river.

BE UNPREDICTABLE
Avoid falling into a rut
by always moving toward the unqualified.
Create and recreate.

BE UNUSUAL
Choose to be exceptional in character.
Let your personality develop richly,
including that which is uncommon.

BE UPHELD
Be kept from sinking
by what you choose to support you.
Know that your survival and existence
is encouraged by love.

BE USEFUL
Be of service.
Make your actions count.
Be helpful.
Be involved.

V

BE VALIANT
In the face of adversity
enlist boldly courageous approaches
and attitudes.
Defend worthiness
with excellence in action.

BE VALID
Be effective in producing the desired results.
Let your authority speak
from your just and well-founded experience.

BE VALOROUS
Be resolute in your bravery.
Forge forward with your purposes.
Defeat injustice with the light of truth.

BE VALUED

Relish your actual and potential qualities.
Enjoy regarding self-esteem to a high degree.

BE VERACIOUS

Identify yourself as one who habitually
speaks the truth.
Truthfulness is a building block for intimacy.

BE VERDUROUS

Be rich in the character of flourishing freshness.
Put on airs of newness about you
and prosper in youthful attitudes.

BE VERSATILE

Be capable of turning easily
from one task to another;
cleverly adaptable.
Let your skills have many applications.

BE VESTED

Incorporate your resources and properties
and protect them
as completely and inalienably yours.

BE VIABLE

Be active and wide awake.
Be capable of living.
Grow and develop your inner and outer life.

BE VIBRANT

Exude excitement in your personality.
Affect others with self-assured energy.
Be electric.

BE VIGILANT

Maintain a careful observance for danger.
Be mindful and take action
to protect what you consider valuable.

BE VIGOROUS

Saturate your character with energetic
vim and vitality.
Choose to be active and robust.
Be powerful and persuasive in your efforts.

BE VIRTUOUS

Represent the best in human nature.
Produce effects
which result from pure motivations,
modest assumptions,
and even temperament.
Be morally excellent
and chaste in your ethical principles.

BE VISIONARY

Explode the insight of your ideas, views,
and schemes.
Revel in your dreams of what can be.

BE VISUAL
See with and without your eyes.
Spark your imagination
with lucid pictures creatively designed by you.

BE VIVACIOUS
Be lively and animated.
Exuberate with the essence of life.
Let your presence rejuvenate those around you.

BE VIVID
Be vibrant with life.
Shimmer with exciting colors
and a compelling presence.
Breathe the freshness of life
into yourself and others.

BE VOCAL

Exercise your voice.
Choose to speak of that which is promising.
Elucidate upon
what you see,
and what you feel.

BE VOLUNTARY

Discover the joy
of undertaking tasks and chores
which provide nourishment for your self-esteem.
The intentional doing of good things
has widespread effects.

W

BE WARM

Enrich your journey
with a friendly disposition.
Act kindly and affectionately
toward those you meet.
Share your lively feelings with sincere emotions.

BE WEALTHY

Recognize worth
in what you already have.
Enjoy your abundance.
Consider its value from within.

BE WELCOME

Make your arrival pleasurable.
Feel yourself being gladly received.
Present yourself as a gift to others.
Let them unwrap you.

BE WELL

Center yourself in the midst
of all that is true, beautiful, and good.
Thrive wholeheartedly
within the kingdom of Being.

BE WELL-ADVISED

Weigh your considerations
with caution, care, and wisdom.
Act upon the congruency of your analysis.
Choose to be wise.

BE WELL-BALANCED

Seek to exist in a state of equilibrium.
See both cause and effect.
Make the necessary adjustments
and arrange your being
into alignment with all that promotes life.

BE WELL-BELOVED

You are respected and honored
by companions traveling with you
in your relation-ships.
Know that you are deeply loved
and embraced with good will.

BE WELL-FED

Maintain proper nourishment
and be prepared for the bright future
you so long for.

BE WELL-FOUNDED

Base your thinking
upon good reasoning and sound information.
Connect your heart and your head.
Align your emotions with your intelligence.

BE WELL-MEANING

Have good intentions.
Proceed from a construct of thought
which promotes the enjoyment
of a meaningful life.

BE WELL-READ

Expose yourself to the thoughts of others.
Develop your imagination
and educate your mind.
Read as much as you can.

BE WELL-ROUNDED

Pursue varied abilities and attainments.
Become fully developed
and maintain balance in your personality.

BE WELL-SPOKEN

If your foot slips, you can recover from your fall.
If your tongue slips,
you may never recover at all.
Express yourself carefully
and with knowledgeable intent.

BE WELL-TIMED

Let the movement of your life
be in motion
with that which is opportune.

BE WELL-WISHING

Think good thoughts of others' well being.
Bless them in your mind
with the emotions in your heart.

BE WHOLEHEARTED

Be honest with yourself.
Be complete in your range of emotions.
Release your total energy and commitment.

BE WILLING

Design your wishes and desires
according to what you decide upon.
Deliberately choose actions
based upon intelligent reflection.

BE WINNING

Set a goal,
gain favor,
reach for your best,
and attain with satisfaction.

BE WIN/WIN

Participate for results
that are mutual in reward.
Prefer games and diversions
where the aim is reciprocal.

BE WISE
Exercise your power of discernment
and judgment.
Know what is known to others and more.
Choose with insight what you do today
to create tomorrow.

BE WISHFUL
Imagine what it's like to be, do,
or have what you long for.
Aspire to ascend the circles of attainment.
Ascribe perfection to yourself.

BE WITHIN
Delicately open your heart.
Explore the wonder of your mind,
and listen to the celestial murmuring
of your soul.

BE WITH IT

Get with the program
and make it something it couldn't have been
without you.
Get on with your life.

BE WITTY

Possess ingenuity in speech and writing.
Permit your understanding
to be amusingly clever in perception
and expression.

BE WONDERFUL

Seek new levels of wonder.
Admire that which seems marvelous
and extraordinary.
Harmonize with the remarkable.

BE WORTHY

Inwardly know
that you possess great merit.
Set the constitution of your character
to extend from a state of value.
onsider goodness to be your strongest asset.

Y

BE YOU

You are the "I AM" within you.
Your memory, understanding, and insight
make up your identity.

BE YOUTHFUL

Embrace a wholesome enjoyment
of freshness and vigor.
Enliven yourself with the eternal qualities
of innocence, curiosity, and vitality.

Z

BE ZANY

Emphasize your personality
with dramatic humor.
Add a sense of fun to your self-image,
and seek to surprise others
with an unexpectedly good nature.

BE ZEALOUS

Express your passions
and devote your intelligence
to diligent efforts.

BE GIVING

Supply copies of this book
to your friends, families, and associates.
Share the illuminating treasures found within,
and bequeath
these mentally enriching heirlooms of thought
to your children through example.

BE INVITED

Submit comments and personal stories of positive
attitudes to: B.B., 607 Corona Street, Suite 274-B,
Denver, CO 80218-3406